T0387662

WHO'S H**OO**? OWLS!

Burrowing Owls

by Rachael Barnes

BELLWETHER MEDIA • MINNEAPOLIS, MN

BLASTOFF! 2 READERS

Blastoff! Readers are carefully developed by literacy experts to build reading stamina and move students toward fluency by combining standards-based content with developmentally appropriate text.

Level 1 provides the most support through repetition of high-frequency words, light text, predictable sentence patterns, and strong visual support.

Level 2 offers early readers a bit more challenge through varied sentences, increased text load, and text-supportive special features.

Level 3 advances early-fluent readers toward fluency through increased text load, less reliance on photos, advancing concepts, longer sentences, and more complex special features.

★ **Blastoff! Universe**

Reading Level

Grade K

Grades 1–3

Grade 4

This edition first published in 2024 by Bellwether Media, Inc.

No part of this publication may be reproduced in whole or in part without written permission of the publisher. For information regarding permission, write to Bellwether Media, Inc., Attention: Permissions Department, 6012 Blue Circle Drive, Minnetonka, MN 55343.

Library of Congress Cataloging-in-Publication Data

Names: Barnes, Rachael, author.
Title: Burrowing owls / by Rachael Barnes.
Description: Minneapolis, MN : Bellwether Media, Inc., 2024. | Series: Blastoff! Readers. Who's hoo? Owls! | Includes bibliographical references and index. | Audience: Ages 5-8 | Audience: Grades 2-3 | Summary: "Relevant images match informative text in this introduction to burrowing owls. Intended for students in kindergarten through third grade"-- Provided by publisher.
Identifiers: LCCN 2023008916 (print) | LCCN 2023008917 (ebook) | ISBN 9798886874136 (library binding) | ISBN 9798886876017 (ebook)
Subjects: LCSH: Burrowing owl--Juvenile literature.
Classification: LCC QL696.S83 B369 2024 (print) | LCC QL696.S83 (ebook) | DDC 598.9/715648--dc23/eng/20230324
LC record available at https://lccn.loc.gov/2023008916
LC ebook record available at https://lccn.loc.gov/2023008917

Editor: Rebecca Sabelko   Designer: Brittany McIntosh

Printed in the United States of America, North Mankato, MN.

Table of Contents

Long-legged Raptors

burrow

Burrowing owls live in
North and South America.
They make homes in **burrows**
in **grasslands** and **deserts**.

4

They are the only **raptors** that live underground!

Burrowing Owl Range

N
W ⭑ E
S

range = ▮

Burrowing owls are small. They are about 10 inches (25 centimeters) tall.

Their **wingspan** only reaches 2 feet (0.6 meters) wide!

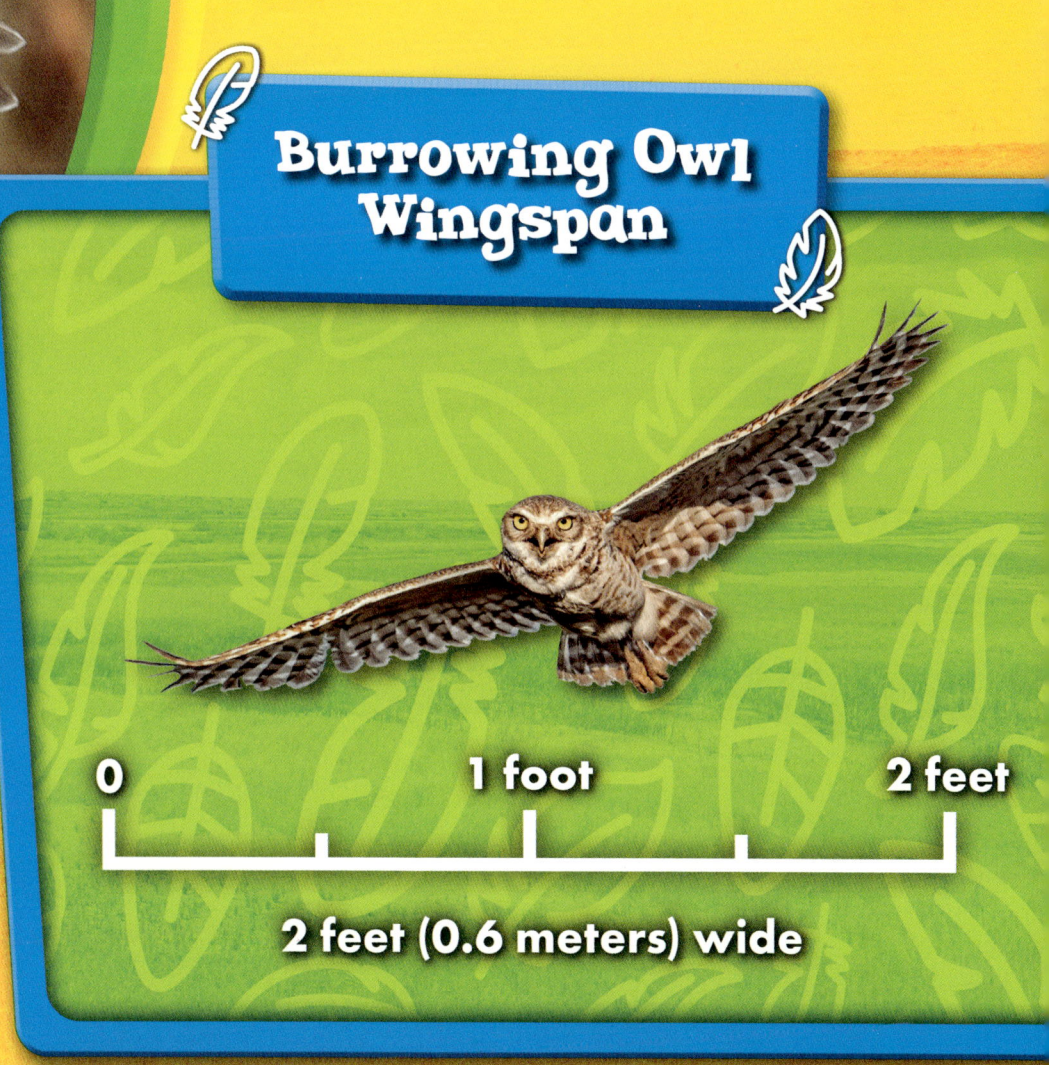

Burrowing Owl Wingspan

0   1 foot   2 feet

2 feet (0.6 meters) wide

They have rounded heads.
Large white eyebrows
rest above their
bright yellow eyes.

bright yellow
eyes

small, sharp
beak

They have small, sharp beaks.

Burrowing owls have
brown feathers with light spots.

Their long legs stick out from their fluffy bodies. Their feet each have four sharp **talons**.

Spot a Burrowing Owl!

large white eyebrows

sharp talons

long legs

11

Racing to Food

Burrowing owls often look for food as the sun goes down. They search from low **perches**.

Sometimes males hunt **rodents** at night. Females may catch **insects** during the day.

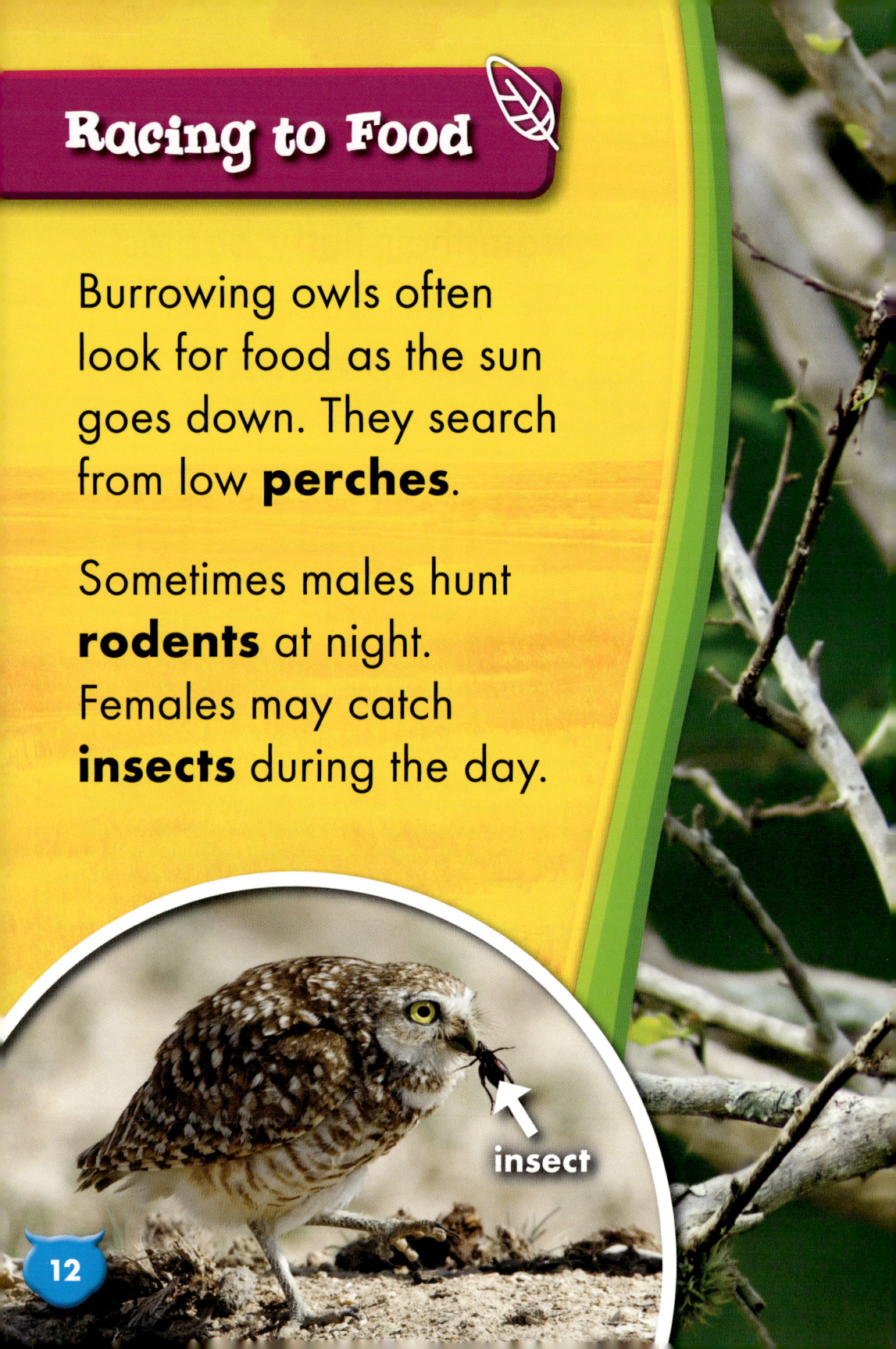

insect

12

Burrowing Owl Food

rodents

insects

perch

13

Burrowing owls fly or run
to chase their **prey**.

They use their sharp talons
to catch their food!

15

Burrowing owls watch for **predators**. They hide in their burrows from hawks and foxes.

predator

owlets

16

Owlets can copy rattlesnake noises. The sounds scare predators away!

17

Beyond the Hunt

Many burrowing owls nest in the same area. They find or make burrows in soft ground.

18

Females lay 2 to 12 eggs in each **clutch**.

clutch

Parents bring food
to their burrows
to feed their young.

Young owls
practice hunting.
They jump on
insects and sticks.
Soon **fledglings**
begin to fly!

fledgling

20

Growing Up

1. egg — 28 to 30 days
2. owlet — 2 to 6 weeks
3. fledgling — around 6 weeks

life span: 6 to 8 years

21

Glossary

burrows—tunnels or holes in the ground used as animal homes

clutch—a group of bird eggs

deserts—dry lands with few plants and little rainfall

fledglings—young owls that have feathers for flight

grasslands—lands covered with grasses and other soft plants with few bushes or trees

insects—small animals with six legs and hard outer bodies; an insect's body is divided into three parts.

owlets—baby owls

perches—places to sit or rest above the ground

predators—animals that hunt other animals for food

prey—animals that are hunted by other animals for food

raptors—large birds that hunt other animals; raptors have excellent eyesight and powerful talons.

rodents—small animals that gnaw on their food; mice, rats, and squirrels are all rodents.

talons—the strong, sharp claws of owls and other raptors

wingspan—the distance from the tip of one wing to the tip of the other wing

To Learn More

AT THE LIBRARY

Emminizer, Theresa. *Swift Snowy Owls*. New York, N.Y.: PowerKids Press, 2022.

Kenney, Karen Latchana. *Prairies*. Minneapolis, Minn.: Bellwether Media, 2022.

Neuenfeldt, Elizabeth. *Elf Owls*. Minneapolis, Minn.: Bellwether Media, 2024.

ON THE WEB

FACTSURFER

Factsurfer.com gives you a safe, fun way to find more information.

1. Go to www.factsurfer.com.

2. Enter "burrowing owls" into the search box and click 🔍.

3. Select your book cover to see a list of related content.

Index

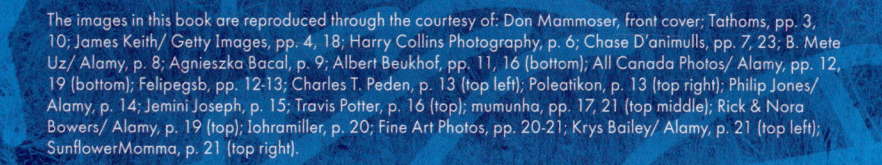

The images in this book are reproduced through the courtesy of: Don Mammoser, front cover; Tathoms, pp. 3, 10; James Keith/ Getty Images, pp. 4, 18; Harry Collins Photography, p. 6; Chase D'animulls, pp. 7, 23; B. Mete Uz/ Alamy, p. 8; Agnieszka Bacal, p. 9; Albert Beukhof, pp. 11, 16 (bottom); All Canada Photos/ Alamy, pp. 12, 19 (bottom); Felipegsb, pp. 12-13; Charles T. Peden, p. 13 (top left); Poleatikon, p. 13 (top right); Philip Jones/ Alamy, p. 14; Jemini Joseph, p. 15; Travis Potter, p. 16 (top); mumunha, pp. 17, 21 (top middle); Rick & Nora Bowers/ Alamy, p. 19 (top); Iohramiller, p. 20; Fine Art Photos, pp. 20-21; Krys Bailey/ Alamy, p. 21 (top left); SunflowerMomma, p. 21 (top right).